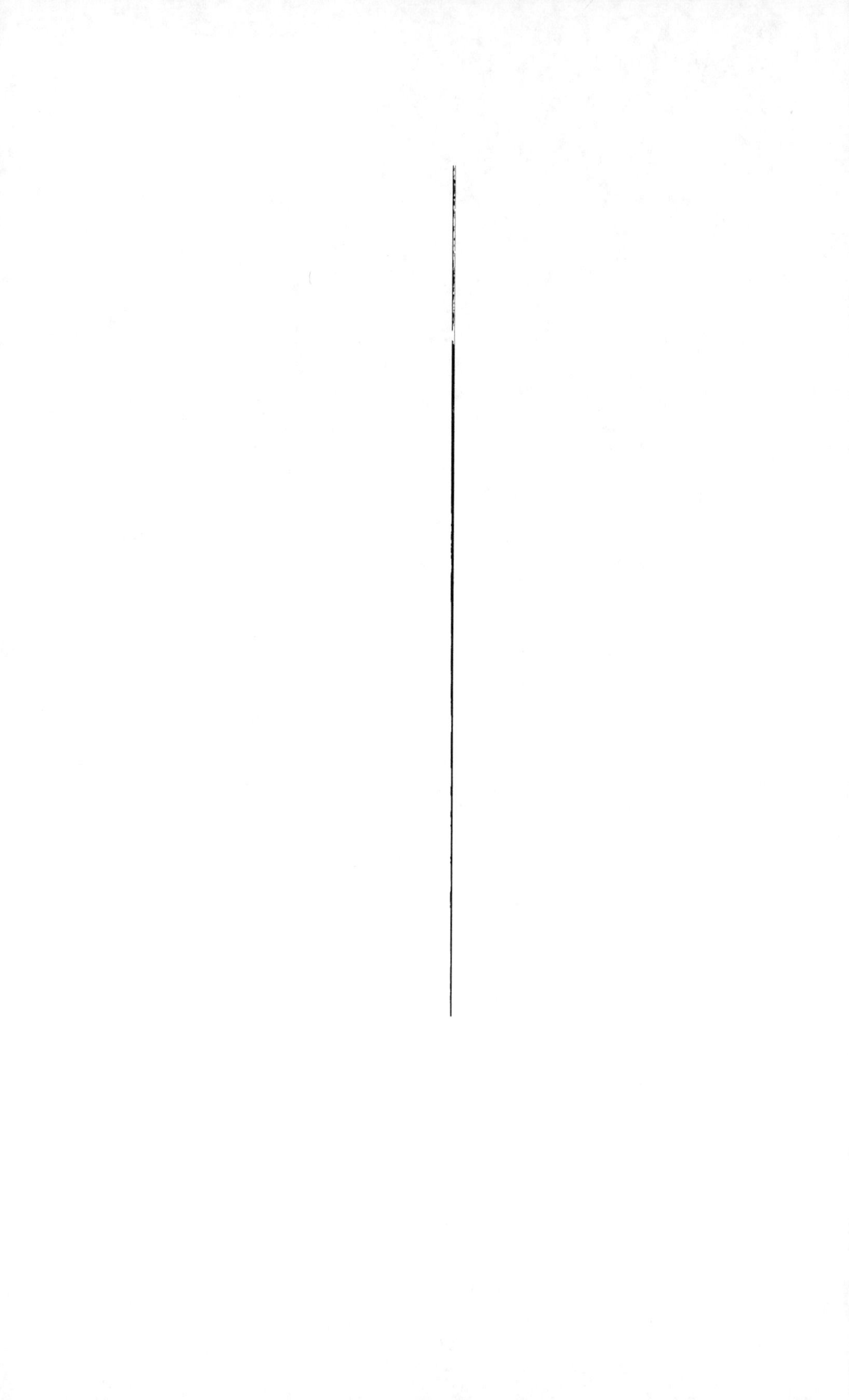

REPORTS ON THE PINGUICO MINES

Reports on the
Properties of
Pinguico Mines Company
in
Guanajuato, Mexico

Covering the Geological,
Metallurgical, Mining and
Milling Features of
these Properties

By

Prof. Robt. T. Hill
of New York

Mr. E. A. Wiltsee, E. M.
of New York

Prof. John A. Church, E. M.
of New York

Mr. A. B. Carpenter, E. M.
of Mexico City

Mr. J. B. Empson, E. M.
of Guanajuato, Mex.

Mr. Geo. W. Bryant
of Guanajuato, Mex.
General Manager of Mines

THE SECURITIES CORPORATION, LTD.
40 Wall Street, New York

Arranged and Printed at
The CHELTENHAM Press
New York

INTRODUCTION

THE six reports contained in this volume will, it is believed, be found to contain all information necessary to an intelligent understanding of every feature connected with the properties under discussion. The authorities quoted have made their investigation independently one of the other, and in every case they have confined themselves strictly to facts and figures.

The result is a collection of documents which cover the geological, metallurgical, and mining and milling conditions which prevail, with precise statements of what these properties are producing to-day, as well as conservative and well-founded estimates of their future possibilities. In securing the services of the gentlemen whose names appear in this volume we have spared no effort or expense, and we ask for their conclusions the careful reading to which the high reputation of these experts entitles them.

We have pleasure in being able to submit such complete and authoritative information, and we have no hesitancy in endorsing every statement contained in the several reports.

THE SECURITIES CORPORATION, LTD.,
40 WALL STREET, NEW YORK

REPORT OF PROF. ROBT. T. HILL

PROFESSOR HILL is an authority on mining geology, second
to none—his examination of mining properties in their early
stages of development, the values of which depended upon
geological condition, have included the well-known properties of
The Greene Consolidated Copper mine at Cananea, Sonora, Mexico;
The Jimulco Mines of Coahuila, Mexico; The Baroteran Coal fields
of Coahuila, Mexico; The Mitchell Copper Mines at La Dicha,
Guerrero, Mexico; and numerous other properties, all of which
have produced great values verifying the anticipations which he
predicted on their geologic conditions.

*"Prof. Robt. T. Hill is a Fellow of the American Geological
Society, Fellow American Association for the Advancement of Science,
member of American Institute of Mining Engineers, President Pelee
Club, member American Geographers' Association, member National
Geographic Society, and member of other societies and technical insti-
tutions.   For some time Professor Hill was lecturer at various colleges
and universities.   He has held many important positions, was Assistant Paleontologist of the Smithsonian Institution ; Geologist of the
United States Geological Survey, 1885–1904; Professor of Geology
at University of Texas ; geologist in charge of United States investigation of underground water in arid regions, and co-operator with
Prof. A. Agassiz in West Indian and Central American explorations,
1895–1905.   For 20 years Professor Hill has been engaged in scien-
tific reconnoissance in Arkansas, Mexico, Central America, and West
Indies and at present is completing his study of Mexican Sierras.   In
1898 he explored for the first time the great canyons of the Rio Grande.
He was the special commissioner of the Geographic Society to study
the Martinique eruptions in 1902."*
—Excerpt from *The Mining World*, September 15, 1906.

Report upon the Properties of

THE PINGUICO MINES COMPANY

By Prof. Robt. T. Hill

INTRODUCTION

THE mines of Guanajuato are so well known in literature and history that it appears unnecessary, in this report, to give other than the briefest account of the camp in general in order to show the exact relations thereto of the property under discussion.

I will confine my report first to the Pinguico Mine proper, to be followed later by geologic and other conditions upon which I formed my opinion.

THE PINGUICO MINE

THE Pinguico Mine is situated about four miles southeast of the center of the City of Guanajuato, with which city it is connected by a good cart road for the entire distance. The City of Guanajuato is located about 250 miles north of the City of Mexico and is reached by direct connection with the Mexican Central Railroad.

The Pinguico Mine is upon a divide which separates the drainage flowing northward into the Town of Guanajuato and about a mile south of the Village of Calderones. It is also immediately to the northwest and adjoins the Carmen Mine, of which it is by nature a part and continuation.

Topographically the ground is a high rounded barren hill constituting the drainage divide between the Guanajuato River, the Rio Cedro, and unnamed creeks flowing southwestward into the plains at the southern end of the Guanajuato mountains. The apex of this hill gives a rising ground of about a thousand feet above the bed of the Cedro Creek to the east, thereby enabling that depth to be obtained along the vein by continuing the horizontal adits of the Carmen Mine into the Pinguico ground, and likewise affording drainage for the mine to this depth.

THE PINGUICO VEIN

THE Pinguico-Carmen vein consists of mineralized fillings of a persistent deep-seated vertical fault fracture zone and replacement rock along them, all more fully described later in this report. In its primary geological elements the Pinguico-Carmen vein is exceedingly simple. It is a typical "fissure vein" faulted and brecciated, impregnated by ascending mineral solutions. The details of this simple type are modified and complicated, however, by the additional susceptibility of the rock material for replacement and by the peculiarity of the ore consisting of an almost liquid black mud which penetrades every lateral crack and fissure.

The movement along this fault line has resulted in the making of a zone of fissure spaces and brecciated interspaces which have served as a suitable channel for the circulation of the ascending mineralizing solutions. The latter have filled the cavities of the fissures, the breccias, and even replaced certain elements of the adjacent rocks with the metallic ores. Therefore, this is a true fissure vein, modified by replacement.

While there is apparently a continuous well-defined and persistent vein of from three to eighteen feet wide, there are parallel fractures within a width of about twenty-five feet which are also more or less mineralized. In places, there are also divergent and convergent fractures.

The width of the vein or lode has not been fully determined. The drifts and shafts through the ore average two meters, but the walls of the ore are nowhere finally delimited by cross-cutting as yet. In the few cross-cuts made, the ore showed a much greater width than two meters, in places going over five meters. In the Carmen extension the minimum width of the vein was three feet, and the miximum eighteen.

The Pinguico vein outcrops at the surface in a northwest-southeast direction and is continuously traced by the workings upon the Carmen ground 1,400 feet and by outcrops and workings in the Pinguico ground for 229 feet, a total of 1,629 feet, all of which is proven to be mineralized, the mineralization continuing to the most northwestwardly breasts of the lower levels of the Pinguico mine workings in that direction.

THE ORES

THE ores of the Pinguico-Carmen mine, like those of the Guanajuato camp in general, consist of a mixture of gold and silver. These occur in association with crumbling sugar quartz in the vein spaces, the brecciated rock, and as replacement in the altered rhyolite country rock. Much, or most of the ore, is in the form of a black mud which seems to permeate and fill every fracture and crevice. This mud is the comminuted country rock and the residuum of the altered rhyolite. Accompanying the mud are many lumps and fragments of more solid rock and spongy quartz, but the material is so soft and easily worked that no blasting is required.

In the Carmen mine, where the same vein has been worked to a greater depth of 250 feet, it is said that the muddy condition of the ores is disappearing and the vein matter is more massive quartz as elsewhere in the Guanajuato District.

DEVELOPMENT

THE present development consists of an exploratory shaft about 430 feet in depth at the southeast end of the Pinguico ground, and a permanent main working shaft in process of sinking near the center of the ground.

The exploratory shaft was started upon fissures encountered in a cross-cut adit or tunnel at a point nearly 300 feet lower than the apex of the hill and 370 feet above the main working level of the Carmen mine, with the intention of intercepting the continuation of the Carmen vein. This point was originally prospected on the Mexican plan by gopher or corkscrew winze to a depth of about 160 feet, after which a straight near-by shaft was started from the adit level, and regular levels running to the northwest were begun at 75, 83, 96, 103, 113, and 125 meters respectively. The 113-meter level connects with the main working level of the Carmen.

The Pinguico vein having previously been developed abundantly and profitably up to the Pinguico line by the Carmen adit, the exploratory shaft upon the Pinguico ground was sunk as near the Carmen workings as possible in order to intercept the continuation of the ore as developed within the Carmen workings. As a result the vein upon the Pinguico ground is at present (May, 1906) developed only upon its end adjoining the Carmen mine, and for a distance of 229 feet to the northwest thereof on the lower levels (125 meters) connecting with the main working adit of the Carmen mine, and still 250 feet above the lower adit of the latter mine, which is now being run toward the Pinguico mine.

Of the levels run northwestward from the shaft along the vein, that at 73 meters had extended 170 feet, the one at 103 meters 348 feet, and the one at 125 meters 229 feet at the time of my examination.

The ends of these drifts and bottoms of the winzes are all continuing in excellent ore.

About 1,500 feet northwest from the present exploratory shaft a new modern three-compartment main working shaft is being sunk from the surface. This will be the future operating center of the mine. At present it is sunk to a depth of about sixty feet and working is rapidly continuing. Two good buildings are erected at this point, and an air-compressor plant and electric hoist were upon the ground and being installed at the time of my visit.

The description of the development of the property as given in the report by G. W. Bryant, dated September 7, 1905, I found to be accurate with the exception, of course, of the additional working which has progressed since it was written.

The present working shaft was originally put down for exploration purposes as a temporary expedient, and will serve its uses well until the mine finds a new outlet to the surface through the well-planned and commodious shaft which is being driven from the surface. When this shaft is completed and the connecting levels are opened it will be well adapted for every possible purpose and complete a chain of perfect ventilation.

VALUES

ALL of the development work above described, except the new shaft, which is off the vein, is entirely in ore, and the Pinguico-Carmen vein carries values throughout its entire length to which it has been developed, now a distance of 1,629 feet, and for a vertical range of 500 feet. Furthermore, the values are continuing and increasing as greater depth is attained and as the workings extend into the Pinguico ground.

The values within the persistent vein are good, but increase and decrease in alternating intervals, so that there are portions corresponding to richer shoots in a regular vein attaining as high as three ounces of gold per ton in some places, while in others the values materially decrease.

This variability in richness of the ore is not an irregularity, but on the other hand a most valuable and encouraging feature, for all mineral veins, as the miner knows, are thus variable, and rich shoots are seldom found in nature to recur so often in any mine as they are found here. Over 1,000 feet of the 1,400 feet of the same vein in the adjoining Carmen mines proved commercially profitable, and five great ore shoots were encountered.

The Pinguico was fortunate in striking one of these shoots in the exploratory shaft, and has been doubly fortunate in already encountering in its drifts another shoot even richer than those formerly encountered, and the faces of the drifts were found in this shoot at the time of my examination. While either of these, if pursued in depth, would constitute a mine, there is every reason, as well as hope, to believe that other rich shoots will be encountered, not only completely across the ground, but as far as the Pinguico-Carmen fault line extends.

The values in this vein up to date in both the Carmen and Pinguico mines have steadily increased with depth. *Vice versa*, the ore shoots become impoverished toward the surface, so that the pay values are seldom encountered until considerable depth has been reached, a condition resembling very much that found in Pachuca, where the ore shoots fade out in value toward the surface.

In 1903 the writer saw the Pinguico mine. Sinking had commenced from the cross-cut tunnel, opening up the well-defined fractures which had, however, but feeble mineralization. Since then sinking continued at this point encountered the continuation of the Carmen vein, and all of the development work has continued in ore.

As the Mexican miners progressed in this work, the ore encountered was extracted and shipped, and, prior to the transfer of the mine to the present owners, in the space of a very short period of time 1,390 metric tons, averaging in value $40.10 per ton U. S. Cy., were shipped, from which all of the mine expenses, besides liberal dividends, were paid.

An average of fifty samples taken at the time of my examination on the 103 and 125 meter levels is $47.68 U. S. Cy. per ton, and some of these run as high as $200. I estimate that in this small developed portion of the mine, assuming the width of the mine should prove to be fifteen feet as indicated by the few cross-cuts run, the total ore in sight (May, 1906) would be over Two and a Half Million Dollars ($2,500,000). This work represents only four months of development, and in consideration of the shortness of this time these results are remarkable.

The headings and bottoms of all the works were in rich ore at the time of my visit, and sample essays therefrom ran over $100 U. S. Cy. per ton.

Up to date, in sinking the shaft and driving the drift levels below the point where ore was first encountered, the average grade has exceeded $40 U. S. Cy. per ton for all the actual ground extracted.

Complete official records of the ore shipments to date from this development work are on file at the offices in Guanajuato.

CONCLUSIONS

THE Pinguico property, notwithstanding the limited development, is a mine of unusual value at present and gives every geological promise of continuing to carry good ore values as development proceeds in the future.

The Guanajuato veins are pre-eminent in the fact that the veins have great extension in depth and in length along the fault fractures. There is no reason whatever for anticipating a discontinuance of the ore in depth or in length as the drifts are driven northwestward upon the Pinguico Vein.

It would not be beyond reasonable possibility to discover ores along the Carmen-Pinguico fault far to the northwest of the Pinguico ground at some early date.*

In view of the geological structure described, it is difficult to prognosticate what conditions will be encountered at the intersection upon the Pinguico ground of the Pinguico Vein and the Pinguico Dike. Inasmuch as the latter follows a great north-south fracture intersecting

* This ground referred to has since been acquired and is to-day owned by the Company.

the vein, and the line of contact of its walls with the rhyolite and tuffs forms a favorable plane for the circulation of solutions, it is very possible that good and large shoots of ore may be encountered at this intersection.

The present bottom of this mine is still in relatively shallow depths and fully 200 feet above the adjacent valley of Cedro Creek. There is every reason and precedent for believing that the Pinguico-Carmen Vein and values will continue in depth. The first reason for this is that the vein is a true deep-seated fissure vein in a district where all the developed mines have demonstrated that the veins carry their values as deep as it has been possible to mine them. There is no reason for anticipating that the Pinguico will prove an exception to this rule.

A second reason is that the downward continuation of the same vein in the adjacent Carmen Mine has already been proven 250 feet below the bottom workings of Pinguico, and still maintains its values.

The ore in sight already developed at shallow depths by the first preliminary shaft at the eastern end of the vein, and at a moderate depth, represents only one-twelfth of the lineal extent of the vein on the company's ground. If the remainder of the vein should hold up the present average as has been maintained through the 2,000 feet of its eastward extension on the Carmen ground, the prospective value of this mine is indeed great.

I find that the development work of the mine has been well planned, and have no suggestions to make for its betterment. The management and conducting of the work seemed also to be most excellent.

All in all considered—the geological conditions, the stable persistence of the vein, the great values exposed in proportion to the limited exploration work, the extent of the adjacent Carmen property (which is a part of the same vein), and the richness of the ores already in sight—I consider the Pinguico mine one of the best that I have ever examined.

GEOLOGY OF THE PINGUICO HILL

THE particular rocks constituting the matrix or country rock of the Pinguico Vein are parts of the general complex of the Guanajuato District, but quite different in material and arrangement from the rocks of the northern part of the mother vein, where the Guanajuato conglomerate and underlying beds are the chief country rocks.

The rocks of the Pinguico Hill consist, as far as known, of beds of the green and white Calderones tuffs (rhyolitic), white rhyolite, and andesite.

The entirely different aspect of these country materials at Pinguico from those of the northern districts may possibly account for the neglect of the Pinguico District by the early miners.

The surface and slopes of the Pinguico-Carmen Hill comprise exposure of bedded tuffs, massive rhyolite or porphyry, and dikes of andesite. The former occurs northeast of the fault line, crossing the property from southeast to northwest, and the last to the southwest thereof, and in the slopes and bluffs toward Cedro Creek.

The rhyolitic rock forms the chief ore matrix of the veins as far as explored. This rock is nearly pure white in color, is largely feldspathic, and contains quartz and mica. This material is in part flow matter and in part dike or intrusion, although upon this point I am not certain.

THE DIKE SYSTEM

UPON the Pinguico ground, and in the immediate area to the northward extending beyond Calderones Village, is a remarkable series of brownish andesitic dikes protruding through the lighter colored rhyolitic tuffs and traceable for long distances through the country. These dikes run in north-south and east-west directions.

A large dike of this character about twenty feet in width, which may be called the Pinguico Dike, commences to outcrop on the Pinguico ground and runs nearly north to the distant Chichindero Peak. Still another, but smaller, east-west dike crosses the Pinguico Dike just south of the Village of Calderones. The largest of these dikes, fully forty feet in width, runs east and west, just north of the Village of Calderones, toward the Cedro Mine.

The dikes are all necessarily of later age than the Calderones tuffs, but they are capped by and hence older than the latest rhyolitic flow of Chichindero Hill, which is related in age to the Carmen rhyolite.

These dikes apparently rise from a great andesitic laccolith of intrusion which is concealed beneath this southern end of the Veta Madre District and which may ultimately be encountered in the lower workings of the mine.

The andesitic dikes, above mentioned, have been thought to have some connection with the mineralization of the Pinguico-Carmen Vein, but my later studies show clearly that the Pinguico-Carmen fault which the mineralization follows clearly cuts across the dikes, indicating that the fissures and mineralization of the veins are probably of later age than the dikes.

THE COUNTRY ROCK

THE country rock of the Pinguico-Carmen Vein, which has an important bearing upon the ore deposition, consists of white rhyolitic material. This rock is composed largely of soluble feldspar, like a similar rock which forms the matrix of most of the great replacement copper bodies of the Sonoran-Arizona Nevada Province. The feldspars of this rock are very decomposable into clay or soaplike substances, known by the Mexicans as "jaboncilla." As a result of this character of the rock, the values are found not only in the vein spaces, but replacing the feldspars in the wall rock itself.

THE PINGUICO-CARMEN FAULT

THE chief geologic and economic feature of the Pinguico and Carmen mines is a persistent deep-seated vertical fault zone with its accompanying fractures, having a direction of N. 40° W. to N. 45° W. Magnetic.

This fault line, which is supposed to branch diagonally from the mother vein at La Union Mine, constitutes the outcrop or creston of the vein, is clearly traceable from the bluffs at the southeast end of the Carmen ground across the surface of the latter and into and across the Pinguico ground to the great north-south andesite dike, where the rhyolite porphyry is brought by faulting in direct contact with the Calderones tuffs. From thence, northwestward, its identity is obscured for about two kilometers as it passes into the andesitic tuffs. The fault again appears at a point northwest of the Village of Calderones and where the ancient mule trail crosses the Calderones Dike, where it is most distinctly displayed N. 45° W. toward the mine of San Prospero on the north side of the Guanajuato camp.

This faulting is also shown underground by the shearing and slipping within the veins themselves, by the brecciated character of the veins, the movement planes of the wall rock, the lenticular swells and pinches of the veins, and upon the surface contacts.

This major fault zone is crossed by complemental minor fractures, and it may prove possible that the numerous richer shoots of ore encountered along the vein occur at the intersection of these two fracture strikes.

It is my present opinion that this fault line is a continuation of one of the hanging wall fractures of the northern half of the mother-vein district, which opinion, however, is subject to modification upon future research.

THE MINES OF GUANAJUATO

THE mines of Guanajuato are so well known in literature * and history that it is hardly necessary to follow the description of the Pinguico ground with more than the briefest account of the camp in general in order to show the exact relation thereto of the property under discussion.

The Guanajuato Mines, occupying an

* See Engineering and Mining Journal, April 14–21, 1904. Engineering Magazine, 1906, and numerous other books and articles of recent years.

area of about 150 square miles, are situated in an isolated group of mountains which rise from the floor of the Mexican plateau, just north of the great volcanic highlands.

In general, the Guanajuato Mountains, rising abruptly above the desert plains of the east and west, now present the aspect of the remnant of an extensive irregular volcanic plateau, greatly dissected by erosion. In a commercial report, like the present, it is impossible to discuss the interesting physiographic history of these mountains.

GENERAL GEOLOGY

THE geological conditions of the Guanajuato District are characterized by every favorable aspect for the occurrence of ores, including extensive fissuring of the country rock, the filling of these fissures with strong and persistent mineralized lodes on a large scale, the presence of a country rock suitable for mineral deposition, and the existence of previous but recent geologic epochs of vast manifestations of igneous activity beneath the area, to which action geologists now admit is due the origin of most of the great mineral lodes of the Cordilleran region.

GEOLOGIC MATERIAL

A GENERAL section of the rock material of the entire district, reading from above downward, is as follows:

BEDDED ROCKS

5. Chichindero rhyolites, rhyolitic lavas with typical flow structure capping Chichindero Hill, the highest eminence of the vicinity of the southern portion of the district, thickness approximately. .200 ft.

4. Calderones tuffs, vast beds of volcanic ash and tuffs of light gray and greenish colors, estimated thickness. .2,100 ft.

3. Clear sandstones, persistent beds of light green laminated water-lain tuffs with occasional reddish laminæ, approximately ....25 ft.

2. The Guanajuato conglomerates,

coarse volcanic conglomerates, largely water-lain and oxidized to a deep red or chocolate color, abundantly exposed in the canyon of Guanajuato, approximate thickness................1,400 ft.

1. Valenciana schist; altered and distorted calcareous shale, and impure limestones constituting the only known marine sediments of the district, outcropping in the footwall district, near Valenciana Mine, thickness unknown.

The Valenciana beds, the so-called schists—the apparent basal rock—are exposed principally in a triangular area to the north of the town, where they constitute the footwall country of the great fault known as the Veta Madre.

INTRUSIVE ROCKS

THE rocks of the above section are mostly volcanic ejecta which have been extruded in past geological time from volcanic vents which have been largely destroyed by subsequent erosion. Intruding these rocks in many places are dikes, laccoliths, and sills of igneous rocks largely of an andesitic nature, and also rhyolitic.

Deep-seated dioritic and granite rocks are also reported in the northwestern extension of the Guanajuato Mountains.

The igneous rocks, both intrusions and ejecta, are widely distributed throughout the district; the former are dikes and stocks of old volcanoes, in some cases laccoliths. The diorites are probably the oldest igneous rocks and occur as dikes and masses in the north-central portion of the area. The western half of the area is largely andesitic, while the eastern half is rhyolitic.

Capping the higher hills around Guanajuato almost everywhere are vast strata of tuffs and agglomerates which largely obscure the older geological formations.

Apparently the oldest and largest body of ejected material is the red conglomerate (Guanajuato formation) which is found on the downthrow side of the Veta Madre in contact with the schists; it consists of a bedded agglomerate over 1,200 feet thick, sometimes pebbly, sometimes angular, alternating with massive homogeneous beds. Much of this con-

glomerate was undoubtedly deposited in water, probably an ancient lake, upon a plain, before the material of the mountains was up-tilted into its present position.

Capping the Guanajuato conglomerate is another great thickness of tuff (the Calderones formation), which is more rhyolitic. It undoubtedly represents several events of extrusion. Some of these tuff beds, from the excess of chloritic coloring, are called the "green tuff": others are of a whiter color. At Chichindera Peak, the highest point near the mother-vein, is a cap rock of rhyolite having a perlitic texture and showing flowing structure, which represents the latest volcanic eruption in the immediate vicinity.

THE FAULT SYSTEM

THE mountains are cut by a number of deep-extending fault systems, the fractures of which, later impregnated by the mineral solutions, now constitute the great mineral veins of the district.

The fault system as an entirety cannot be accurately or finally described until the district is mapped and more thoroughly studied. The major fault system is the great rupture of the Veta Madre. This has a trend of N. 40° W. This fault zone has a total downthrow of from 1,200 feet to 2,000 feet to the west and is composed of many lines of fracture and movement in parallel or subparallel directions lacing and interlacing with one another, constituting the so-called footwall, hanging and intermediate veins. Parallel to this principal fault zone are other fault zones, conspicuous among which are those of the La Luz, Santa Rosa, Pinguico, and Peregrina districts. Complemental to this major direction of faulting there are cross-fractures with an average trend of N. 60° W., as at La Central Mines.

At the foot of the western slope of the mountains there is apparently a line of present fracture from which breaks forth a series of hot springs (at Silao, at the foot of Cubilete, and at the foot of Gigante); these are said to be depositing mineral sulphides.

THE MOTHER-VEIN

THE Guanajuato area as a whole comprises three distinct mining sub-districts, consisting first of the mother vein proper, which extends in a northwest-southeast direction for seven miles through the City of Guanajuato. This is flanked by two outlying districts. The one to the east embraces the Santa Rosa and Peregrina groups; that to the west is known as the La Luz District.

The mother-vein district proper, near which the Pinguico Mine is located, consists of the belt of faulted country from one-half a mile to a mile in width along which are situated the groups of historic mines which have made Guanajuato famous. The oldest and largest of these are along the northern half of the belt; about the middle of the vein is situated the Town of Guanajuato. South of the town are also many important mines.

This mother-vein district consists primarily of a wide zone of mineralized faulting. The mineralization has followed the great fractures of the faulting and its accompanying shear zones resulting in veins with shoots and bodies of ore of unusual extent and richness.

This zone has a width of from 100 to 400 feet, and the whole width is frequently an alternation of quartz veins and country rock. These veins, usually of tremendous size, are known as the footwall, middle, and hanging wall veins. The fractures are filled with quartz and calcite gangue, sometimes enclosing brecciated country rock.

The total length of the portion of the Veta Madre which has been worked is about seven miles, between the Esperanza Mine at the northwest and the Cardones Mines at the southeast. Of this distance about one-third, at least, may be said to be still unexplored. The northern half is accredited with a production of $600,000,000, principally above the 1,000-foot level.

The extension of this vein south of Guanajuato, or rather south of the Sirena Mine, has not been ascertained definitely or accurately, but its course, as is generally accepted, is that laid down upon the current maps.

The Pinguico-Carmen vein is probably a part of the hanging-wall system of the Veta Madre, just west of and near the southern end of its known extension. Strange to say, this vein is one overlooked by the early miners and is therefore practically virgin ground in the Guanajuato District. The vein presents several interesting variations in detail different from the older mines.

Very truly yours,

(Signed) ROBT. T. HILL.

New York, May 22, 1906.

REPORT OF MR. E. A. WILTSEE, E.M.

Mr. E. A. Wiltsee is a Mining Engineer of international reputation. He was formerly assistant to Mr. John Hays Hammond in South Africa; Superintending Engineer for The Consolidated Gold Fields of South Africa, Ltd.; and more recently Resident Manager for the North American continent of The Venture Corporation, Ltd., of London. This last connection he resigned in 1905 in order to devote his time to his private mining interests, which had assumed large proportions in California, Mexico, and South Africa.

Inasmuch as the well-known "Esperanza" mine of El Oro, Mexico, and the "Dolores" mine of Chihuahua, Mexico, were brought out by this engineer, much importance is attached to his highly favorable report upon Pinguico.

Report upon the Properties of
THE PINGUICO MINES COMPANY
By Mr. E. A. Wiltsee, E.M.

Situation—Extent—Accessibility—Mineral Horizon—The Vein—Development Work—Character of the Ore—Discussion of the Ore Body—Mining, Etc.—Measurement of Ore Bodies—Tonnage and Values—Net Values in Sight—Milling and Extraction—Equipment—Further Development—Management—Values and Methods of Sampling—Conclusions.

I herewith submit my report upon the properties of the Pinguico Mines Company, together with the following appendices:

1. Longitudinal-vertical section showing location of the various ore blocks and samples taken.

2. Plan of the underground workings.

3. Longitudinal-vertical section showing the Pinguico and the Carmen underground workings combined.

4. Tabulations showing the ores shipped from the Pinguico Mine to the Nayal Mill, La Central Mill, and the Smelters.

SITUATION

THE property of the Pinguico Mines Company is situated three miles east of the City of Guanajuato, on a comparatively high, rolling hill.

EXTENT

THE property comprises five separate mines having an aggregate area of 121.52 pertenencias, equivalent to 300 acres. These five claims give an extent along the vein of 2,500 meters (8,200 ft.).[1]

The Company also owns a mill site situated in the Cedro Valley, distant one kilometer (⅝ mile), where the new 200-ton mill will be erected. This mill site possesses excellent facilities and is so situated that all ore can be conveyed, by short aerial tram 3,300 feet in length, direct from the "Fortuna" shaft (the main working shaft of the property).

ACCESSIBILITY

THE mine is reached by a good wagon road eight miles in extent from the terminus of the Mexican Central Railway at Marfil, the said wagon road traversing the City of Guanajuato. Freight rates are consequently reasonable, the cost of transportation from railroad to mine being $4.00 per ton, and for ore from mine to railroad $2.00 per ton.

By the extension of the railroad into the City of Guanajuato, now in progress, the distance from the terminal to the mine will be reduced to four miles, and freight rates to and from the mine to $2.40 and $1.20, respectively.

MINERAL HORIZON

THIS consists of rhyolite, andesite breccias and tuffs, and the Guanajuato conglomerates. The vein is a fault replacement in the rhyolite. For a portion of the distance the outcrop of the fissure occurs in a contact between the rhyolites and the overlying andesites; in depth it passes entirely into the rhyolite.

This formation is also extensively diked and presumably the mineralization has been effected to a certain extent through these occurrences, although this fact has not been actually demonstrated in the underground workings as yet.

THE VEIN

THE Pinguico vein is formed by a persistent vertical fault fracture in which mineralized fillings and replacements have occurred. It is a true fissure vein with replacement features highly developed and was undoubtedly mineralized by ascending mineral solutions from depth. Its characteristics indicate permanence and persistence both laterally and downward.

(For detailed description of its geological features see Prof. Robt. T. Hill's comprehensive report.)

The course of the vein is northwest and southeast, and it stands almost vertical, dipping slightly toward the northeast. It is large in size, increasing in depth, as far as proved by the lowest workings of the mine. Its persistence laterally is remarkable, the present ore body being developed to a length of 215 meters (705 ft.) in the Pinguico ground with practically no break in values. In the upper workings of the mine the pay ore in the vein has an average width of from $1\frac{1}{2}$ to 2 meters (4.8 to 6.5 ft.). This width rapidly increases and the 125-meter (407-ft.) level shows a width of pay values from 2 to 9 meters (6.5 to 32.5 ft.), with an average of about 4.9 meters (15.9 ft.) for its entire length at date.

DEVELOPMENT WORK

WHILE the outcrop of the vein is discovered at intervals on the surface, no values have as yet been found there. The development of the property was undertaken and prosecuted on account of the showing in the adjoining "Carmen" Mine, which the Guanajuato Consolidated Mining & Milling Company controls. It was certain that in its course the Carmen vein would pass through the Pinguico property; consequently operations were begun to sink through the barren capping in order to disclose the ore body in depth; a cross-cut tunnel was driven to intersect the course of the vein, and when this was encountered a shaft was sunk from the tunnel in close proximity to the vein. For a time this shaft was barren, but pay ore was finally encountered at a depth of 53 meters (173 ft.) below the tunnel.

While all present development is being done from this interior shaft (called the "South" shaft) an excellent new three-compartment timbered shaft is being sunk close to the course of the vein, in its extent 577 meters (1,875 ft.) to the northwest and about 800 feet from the present northernmost workings. This "Fortuna" shaft has now attained a depth of 82 meters (268 ft.) and has passed through the overlying andesite at a depth of 70 meters (220 ft.) from surface. It is now in rhyolite. It is the intention to make it the permanent working shaft of the mine.

The present development of the mine to be hereinafter described has been, of course, made from the interior shaft above mentioned. The vein was cut in the tunnel at a depth of 58 meters (188 ft.) below surface. Levels were run out at depths of 73 meters (237 ft.), 103 meters (335 ft.), and 125 meters (407 ft.) below the tunnel level; consequently the 125-meter level has a depth of 183 meters (595 ft.) below surface.

The 73-meter level has a length of 53 meters (172 ft.) and while some ore of good grade was found near the shaft, the remainder is in poor ground. This level was practically above the ore-bearing zone.

The 103-meter level has been driven 135 meters (439 ft.) from the shaft. It is in pay milling ore for its entire distance.

The 125-meter level has now been driven 215 meters (705 ft.) from the shaft. It is practically in high-grade ore for its entire distance, with the exception of two short, narrow places in the vein. Four raises connect this present lowest level) with the 103-meter (335-ft.) level, and two other raises are being rapidly advanced. Furthermore, two intermediate levels have been driven in between, the lower of which has an extent of 135 meters (439 ft.) and the upper 65 meters (212 ft.) in length.

At the date of examination the most important points of development were:

the No. 1 and No. 2 winzes being sunk below the 125-meter (407-ft.) level, and from the bottoms of which it is the present intention to drive the next lowest level at a depth of 21 meters (68 ft.) below the 125-meter level. These winzes are now down 16 meters (52 ft.) below the level and are in high-grade ore for their entire depth and would seem to show that the ore body is increasing in size and richness as it is sunk upon. The breast of the 125-meter (407-ft.) level shows high-grade ore, which speaks well for the continuance of the ore body toward the north.

CHARACTER OF THE ORE

THE Pinguico ore contains gold and silver, the values occurring in the relative proportions of 25 per cent. of gold to 75 per cent. of silver, although the gold content is increasing in depth. The ore comprises a soft quartz in the vein spaces, together with a brecciated rock mineralized by replacement, and also replacements and consequent mineralizations in the altered country rock. The entire vein filling is in a crumbled condition due to movements of crushing and comminuting that have taken place in the vein material. A noteworthy characteristic is the soft, black mud that forms a considerable portion of the ore and which permeates all the crevices and interstices in the vein. A lighter colored mud frequently contains the richest values in the vein. These muds are resultant from the attrition of the vein filling and softer quartz. The entire vein is consequently quite soft and broken and is easily worked, admitting of unusual rapidity of development work and of easy and cheap mining.

DISCUSSION OF THE ORE BODY

IN considering this mine, the points of the greatest interest are as to the continuance of the present ore body in depth, and its further extent to the northwest.

The ore body exposed in the Pinguico Mine does not extend to surface, although it shows great persistence laterally, apparently increasing in value and strength in its extent northwest. In the adjacent "Carmen" property, the ore bodies of which appear to be extensions to the south, the same failure to extend to the surface is also observed. As the workings of the two mines are connected through, the ore occurrence can be considered as one and the same. In the southern portion of the Carmen Mine the ore bodies failed to show much extent in depth. A first glance at the ore bodies as exposed in the two properties would appear to indicate a chimney-like occurrence of ore having persistent lateral extent, but cut off above and below, descending at a gentle angle as it trends northwest through the Pinguico property, its highest point being in the southern portion of the Carmen ground; but the deep winzes in the Pinguico Mine disprove this theory, as the best and richest showings to-day are in the bottoms of these winzes, and the ore body shows better values at all points in depth throughout the Pinguico Mine. The continuity of the ore body laterally is remarkable, the ore in the Carmen property extending for 460 meters (1,500 ft.) and in the Pinguico property for 215 meters (700 ft.), a total of 675 meters (2,200 ft.) with the farthest point north (the breast of the 125-meter Pinguico level) in rich pay ore and strong as to width and persistent features. It would seem that this ore body has received its mineralization from some point to the northwest and that its progress would persist thither in size and richness for an indeterminate distance.

A noteworthy fact that is of the greatest importance in predicating continuing values in depth, is the encountering of good ore in the Lower Carmen Tunnel now being driven in that property and at present within 400 feet of the Pinguico line. This tunnel is 62 meters (202 ft.) lower than the 125-meter level of the Pinguico Mine.

From the present showing in the bottom of the Pinguico winzes and in the face of this Carmen tunnel, there would seem to be little doubt that the Pinguico ore body would continue with its present size and values to at least the level of this Lower Carmen Tunnel. While this is as yet, of course, not absolutely proved, still all appearances would indicate that this will be the case.

Taking into consideration these facts, it would seem that the Pinguico ore occurrence is not a lateral chimney, but on the contrary the original vein enrichment would seem to have come from depth and that it will continue in depth to an undetermined extent, which can only be proved by the development of the property. And it would appear as if this ore body for some reason was capped, or at least did not come to surface, and that the ore occurrence in the Carmen property was an arm from the main ore body which found its way along some avenue of least resistance from the main source in the Pinguico property.

MINING, ETC.

THE comparatively soft and crumbling nature of this ore body, already referred to, makes development work and mining comparatively easy. In driving levels, as much as 2 meters (6.5 ft.) a day is frequently attained; and when it comes to stoping ore for the mill on a large scale, corresponding ease in extraction will be found. In the portion of the property now opened, the ore is so easily mined that it is only occasionally necessary to use dynamite. This will reduce the cost of mining and also development to a comparatively low figure, the only additional expense being the necessity of timbering the levels securely. In commenting upon this aspect of the mine, it was observed that all this timbering work is carefully and well handled, and the mine is in excellent and safe condition throughout.

As to the method of stoping, or in other words extracting ore in large quantities for the mill, no definite decision has as yet been arrived at, but in my opinion the method frequently employed which gives good results, namely, keeping the stopes filled with ore as the face is attacked and only drawing off the surplus so that the miners work on the broken ore, will be adopted. This method always gives safety in holding the walls until the broken ore is withdrawn from the stope, after which, of course, the walls are allowed to come together without impairing the safety of the mine, the levels being fully protected.

MEASUREMENT OF ORE BODIES

IT was comparatively easy to arrive at a close and accurate estimate of ore in sight, on account of the several intermediate levels and the small blocks into which the ore bodies have been cut up by means of numerous cross-cuts and raises. The entire mine has been divided up into parallelogram blocks which were sampled on three or four sides. The nature of the ore has lent every facility to easy sampling, and the samples have been taken out at close intervals. On account of the width of the ore body being considerably greater in many places than the workings have proved, in my opinion the measured-up territory, when stoped, will yield a considerably greater tonnage than shown by the careful estimate hereinafter following. Consequently the estimates given in this report will be found by actual working to be on the safe side.

It is but right to state that on account of the small portion of the total territory as yet opened up by development work on this property—which, however, makes an excellent showing—it is hardly fair to the mine to make any measurement of ore in sight at this time. On account of the persistent features of the ore body in depth already referred to, it has been deemed safe to allow ten meters below present faces in computing ore in sight. As the ore body did not show such positive extent upward, in only one block has any allowance been made above present faces. The mine is putting ore in sight so rapidly that the amount herein reported can only be taken as a temporary figure and one which fits the case at this day and date only. When the property was taken over by the present owners on the 22d day of April, 1906, it was estimated by their engineers that there was in sight in the mine not over $250,000.00. To-day, six months later, this amount has been increased to over two million dollars. It is impossible to predict what the outcome of another six months or year of development work will be, and the only procedure will be to add to the figures given in this report the new blocks of ore as rapidly as they are developed in the mine. One entire block (N) has been added since my examination of the property commenced ten days ago, and, furthermore, every meter that is sunk in the rich No. 1 or No. 2 winze, as long as the ore continues to show the values now being found, will add from $40,000 to $50,000 to the total ore in sight in the mine, while lateral advances will add still further values.

In this connection it must not be overlooked that, as already stated, the Lower Carmen level is rapidly approaching the Pinguico boundary and will be continued through the Pinguico ground, giving a depth of about 62 meters (205 ft.) below the present lowest (or 125-meter) level. Should the vein continue in size and value to this level throughout, the ore reserves and consequent net ore in sight will be considerably more than doubled.

TONNAGES AND VALUES

Blocks	Tons	Average Value Per Ton	Gross Value (U. S. Cy.)
A	800	$8.36	$6,688.00
B	2,065	10.15	21,909.00
C	1,084	11.27	12,214.00
D	7,286	26.38	192,215.00
E	9,880	53.83	531,840.00
E-1	717	53.83	38,596.00
F	4,287	35.00	150,045.00
G	3,148	27.55	86,727.00
H	3,755	30.58	114,828.00
I	3,776	23.27	87,867.00
J	1,501	59.45	89,234.00
	662	19.12	12,667.00
K	9,377	23.10	216,609.00
	5,736	63.49	364,179.00
L	3,180	20.00	63,600.00
M	1,070	58.85	62,970.00
N	2,353	21.13	49,718.00
Totals	60,677	$34.64	$2,101,906.00

The foregoing tabulation gives the ore in sight at the present date. It will be noticed that it equals 60,677 tons with an average value of $34.64, the total gross ore in sight amounting to $2,101,906.

Considering that the property has been in the hands of the Guanajuato Development Company but six months—almost half of which time was devoted to preparing the mine for development work—the result is remarkable.

In arriving at the above results, it should be borne in mind that in this method of computation the widths of the vein at the points below the 125-meter level have been reduced to the exact widths shown to date in the winzes (2 meters); but as these winzes are in ore on all sides and as no cross-cuts have yet been run to reach the walls, much greater widths of vein will be proved and will materially add to the estimate of values above given. Until the cross-cuts are driven and the exact widths proved, I confined my results to the actual widths so far exposed. As these lowest blocks are the richest in the mine, these additions will make a considerable difference in the total values. These additions, practical mining men might feel justified in assuming; but as an engineer, I am restrained in my calculations to the actual widths at present shown.

By looking at the map it will be noticed that the ore in the upper workings is much poorer than below; thus blocks "A," "B," and "C" show an average of $8.00, $10.00, and $11.00 respectively; "D," "H," "I," situated above the 125-meter and below the 103-meter level, show ore values running from $20.00 to $40.00 per ton, while blocks "E," "K," and "M" give values running between $50.00 and $60.00 per ton. It will be noticed that block "K" is divided into ore of two grades. The 5,736 tons, averaging $63.49, is the ore exposed by the drives, while the lower-grade ore, amounting to 9,377 tons of an average value of $23.10, is the ore exposed in the numerous cross-cuts outside of the rich portion of the vein, which still has excellent milling values.

In this connection it is significant that the 125-meter level for its entire length of 215 meters (705 ft.) shows an average of over $50.00 U. S. Cy. per ton for the full width of the drift (2 meters or 6¼ ft.). The milling width, or width that would include all the milling ore on this level, is much wider, averaging 4.9 meters (15.9 ft.) throughout.

NET VALUES IN SIGHT

IN calculating the net values from the gross, an extraction of 90 per cent. is taken with a deduction of 5 per cent. for taxes and a total operating cost for mining and milling of $4.00 per ton. The details of the various blocks are then as follows:

Blocks	Tons	Net Average Value Per Ton	Net Value (U. S. Cy.)
A	800		$2,510.00
B	2,065		10,472.00
C	1,084		6,007.00
D	7,286		135,200.00
E	9,880		415,203.00
E–1	717		30,101.00
F	4,287		111,140.00
G	3,148		61,559.00
H	3,755		83,157.00
I	3,776		60,022.00
J	1,501		70,291.00
	662		8,162.00
K	9,377		147,664.00
	5,736		282,729.00
L	3,180		41,658.00
M	1,070		49,559.00
N	2,353		33,096.00
Totals	60,677	at $25.52 =	$1,548,530.00

It will thus be noticed that the tonnage now in sight, namely, 60,677 tons, gives an average net value of $25.52 per ton, and a total net value of ore in sight to date of $1,548,530.00. As elsewhere stated, this is rapidly being added to and can only be taken as representing the net ore in sight at the date of this report.

MILLING AND EXTRACTION

IN almost all reports made upon mines there is an opportunity for discrepancy or error in computing the mill extraction that can be obtained upon the ore in sight in the mine, as it is usually impossible to predict the exact percentage of the values that will be extracted, and in a great many instances the milling process fails to treat the ore with success. In the present case, however, all error is eliminated from the fact that the ore from all over the mine is at present being treated in cyanide mills, with the result that the extraction that can be obtained on the ore is absolutely proved by months of treatment of the same. The Pinguico Mine is fortunate in this regard from another reason, namely, that in constructing their new 200-ton mill, now being built, the treatment of the ore has been thoroughly studied and defined, and the mill that will be erected will not only be the one that is best adapted to the treatment of the ores of the mine, but it can be confidently predicted what the percentage of extraction will be. It might seem to one reading this report that a high percentage of extraction has been adopted in figuring the net values of the Pinguico ores; but as these results have been obtained after six months of careful milling and the figures proved by the actual weighing up of the bullion and concentrates, the writer has no hesitancy in adopting these values as safe in this connection. In all probability the new mill—which will be especially adapted to the treatment of these ores—will secure a slightly higher extraction than is now obtained in the "Nayal" and "La Central" mills, which are run on these ores, but which are in reality merely custom mills undertaking the treatment of the various ores of the camp, with no special adaptation to any. There is appended hereto a tabulation of the entire ore shipments from the mine, including the ore shipped to both these mills, which shows the tonnage and values. These milling results may be summed up as follows: in the last four months about 2,000 tons have been treated by the method known as "concentration and cyaniding." The mill-grade ore from the mine has varied ordinarily from $20.00 to $30.00 U. S. Currency value. It is thoroughly representative, as it has come from all portions of the mine development work. A concentrate of an average value of $1,500.00 U. S. Cy. is produced from the Wilfley tables, a second concentrate of an average of grade of about $550.00 U. S. Cy. being produced from the canvas tables. These concentrates are immediately shipped to the smelters and are eagerly sought for on account of their high grade. The sands and slimes, after passing over the concentrating tables, are treated by cyanide, with the result that the mill is giving the high extraction of 90 per cent. of the silver and 95 per cent. of the gold values contained in the ore, from which there must only be deducted the freight and treatment charges on the concentrates. The above recoveries are most satisfactory and may be taken at 90 per cent. of the entire content of the ore.

It has not been found expedient, with the present limited milling facilities, to ship the high-grade ore to the above-named mills, and at the present time ore having a grade of over $50.00 a ton is being shipped to the smelters direct. When the mine is equipped with its own mill, it is not the intention to continue this practice of shipping ore to the smelters, and this would only take place provided ore of exceptionally high grade is encountered which would be too rich to mill.

EQUIPMENT

THE present equipment of the property comprises the following: A complete installation at the "Fortuna" shaft, including head-gear, a 30-H.P. double-drum electric hoist, substantial buildings, and complete equipment for sinking. The "South" or interior shaft is sunk from the cross-cut tunnel 450 ft. long. It is a vertical shaft, equipped with a 20-H.P. single-drum electric hoist, and an electric pump installed on the 125-meter (407-ft.) level handles the water with ease. At the mouth of the cross-cut tunnel are the dwellings, office, storehouse, and transformer house, all constructed of masonry, and large ore-storing and sorting sheds. The permanent levels in the mine and the cross-cut tunnel are laid with suitable tracks. The No. 2 winze is being sunk below the 125-meter level with its separate 10-H.P. electric hoist.

The additional equipment which is now being rapidly established at the mine consists of a new 50-H.P. electric hoist in the "South" shaft, now being raised to surface, and permanent offices and dwellings, in addition to the new 200-ton mill and aerial tramway connecting same with the "Fortuna" shaft. The streak by itself. This has been done

work is now under construction, and when completed will give the mine an ideal installation.

FURTHER DEVELOPMENT

THE management of the mine is pursuing a wise course in extending the present 125-meter level, which is advancing at the rate of 40 to 50 meters (130 to 165 ft.) per month, and also in pushing in the Lower Carmen Tunnel as rapidly as possible. The "Fortuna" shaft will soon be at such a depth that it can be connected with the 125-meter level; and with these various points of attack there will be no hindrance to such development (provided the ore bodies continue in depth and lateral extent, as they have every present indication of doing) that a remarkable increase to the ore in sight in the mine will be accomplished in a short period.

The extent of the ore body, measured from the Carmen boundary, is at present about 215 meters (705 ft.). The total extent of territory in the Pinguico claims will give the vein in their boundaries a length of 2,500 meters (8,200 ft.). It will be noted that only a small fraction of the extent of the property has as yet been developed. This gives a great opportunity for the discovery and blocking out of additional ore in the exploration of the vein in its northwesterly course.

MANAGEMENT

THE operation of this property since its acquisition, and the present condition of the mine, reflect great credit upon all connected with it—the General Manager, Consulting Engineers, and Superintendents. The mine is well mapped and the assay plans carefully compiled and kept up-to-date.

VALUES AND METHODS OF SAMPLING

IN a mine where the various strata vary so widely in grade and the ore is so comparatively rich, great care should be used in sampling each throughout this mine, and the assays plotted are really built up from a careful sampling of the vein in its various sections. Ordinary samples in ore of this richness and variability would not give accurate results. Consequently in sampling this property, instead of the ordinary trench, a large section of the vein is taken down, with the result that samples usually weigh 100 lbs. and over. Consequently it can be said that the results are accurate and safe. Where waste occurs within the vein in bunches or small horses, such portions were included in the samples. The large samples were broken down to hazel-nut size and carefully quartered. Many portions of the mine have been sampled and resampled, in order to check results. As all samples have been cut from new faces, there has been but little opportunity for error, as in the case of filling or dump samples.

GOLD CONTENTS: In computing values for ore, I have taken 1 gram of gold=66c., equivalent to gold at $20.67 per ounce.

SILVER CONTENTS: I have taken 1 gram=2c., equivalent to 62.6c. per ounce.

All values stated in this report are in United States Currency; all tonnages of the metric ton of 2,200 pounds.

In calculations of distances, the meter has been taken as equivalent to $3\frac{1}{4}$ feet.

CONCLUSIONS

THE Pinguico Mine is the most remarkable development of recent years in the Camp of Guanajuato.

Its exceptional features are readily perceived, and may be briefly summed up as follows:

Its ores are of higher grade than that of any producing mine of the camp, with an average throughout of $34.64 U. S. Cy. per ton.

The unusual character of its vein admits of: FIRST, great rapidity in development, and, SECONDLY, cheap mining, both of which are most important features.

From months of actual treatment, its ores give unusually high percentage of extraction, namely, over 90 per cent.— proved beyond all doubt.

The vein is large and of exceptional persistence. Ore bodies without a break and having a lateral extent of 215 meters (705 ft.) of high-grade ore are rarely met with.

This persistence and continued increase of the ore values in depth is as noteworthy as it is gratifying. Appearances would tend to show that the mine has only opened up the upper and poorer portion of an extensive ore body of unusual richness and length.

It must be remembered that this report does not in any way limit the ore values in the property, but, on the contrary, each week's development work will increase these figures rapidly, and this increase will continue for an indefinite time to come.

The total values in sight to-day have been practically developed and placed in sight by the work of the last four months. Taking this fact into account, it can be readily seen what the next six months may bring forth, with additional facilities for development.

The amount of water to be handled is small, and the mine has all facilities of electric power for the purposes of mining and milling.

It is favorably situated for operation, with its main shaft upon the course of a slowly rising hill, and an excellent mill site near at hand to which the ore can be easily transported.

The mine has easy railroad communication, and its proximity to a large city insures abundant labor.

Taking into account the above facts, this property is strongly recommended as a sure and safe investment. It is a sound business as well as a mining proposition, and is in capable hands.

Finally, attention is particularly called to the probabilities for addition to its values in sight, which from all appearances will take place in the next few months. It must be borne in mind that the values hereinabove given are absolute as of the present day and date only. It is the increase that cannot be predicted which marks the future for this mine, and all indications are that this increase will be rapid and of large extent.

Respectfully submitted,

(Signed) E. A. WILTSEE, E.M.

Guanajuato, Mex., Oct. 26, 1906.

APPENDIX NO. 4 TO E. A. WILTSEE'S REPORT
October 22d, 1906

ORE SALES OF THE PINGUICO MINE, GUANAJUATO, MEXICO
SUMMARY

Date, 1904	Weight: Tons (Kilos)	Average Value Per Ton (U. S. Cy.)	Value in U. S. Cy.
January to May	36.480	$21.08	$706.09
June	52.033	22.11	1,150.21
July	67.276	26.05	1,752.78
August	50.479	29.70	1,499.40
September	38.268	25.05	958.79
October	201.234	32.39	6,518.08
November	53.313	38.57	2,056.42
December	51.509	34.37	1,770.48
1905			
January	19.171	15.23	291.93
February	27.652	85.00	2,350.35
March	69.886	68.66	4,798.23
May	101.716	48.68	4,951.90
June	210.091	44.44	9,337.31
July	238.246	44.38	10,573.93
August	173.042	40.29	6,971.66
September	29.774	129.75	3,863.06
October	24.574	102.24	2,512.66
November	19.834	86.19	1,709.41
December	59.589	64.85	3,864.64
1906			
January	187.465	42.18	7,907.39
February	249.541	47.42	11,835.50
March	284.606	37.70	10,729.62
April	71.945	20.68	1,487.94
May	206.900	28.13	5,820.68
June	491.830	36.15	17,779.64
July	536.817	25.93	13,924.15
August	766.522	27.91	21,395.81
September	1,161.151	33.02	38,344.40
	5,480.994	$35.92	$196,362.48

REPORT OF PROF. J. A. CHURCH, E.M.

Report upon the Properties of
THE PINGUICO MINES COMPANY
By Prof. John A. Church, E.M.

The Mine—Ore Shipped—The New Mill—Mining and Milling Costs—Pinguico Vein—Characteristics of the Mine—Mean Values of Samples—History of Pinguico Vein—Faulting Movements—Leaching—Permanence of Vein—Summarization—Present Condition—Profits.

THE MINE

THE Pinguico Mine is opened in a vein which lies in the ground of two separate properties, the Carmen and the Pinguico. There is a continuous ore body 2,000 feet long which is divided by the common boundary line of the two mines. In this ore there are two short lengths when the vein narrows and the grade is low, but in the mining sense this ore is continuous. Besides this there was a separate body in the Carmen, 400 feet south of the first mentioned, which was about 250 feet long and reached to the surface 140 feet above. This it the only real outcrop of ore on the whole vein, which is covered for the most part by later formations. Thus there has been a length of 2,250 feet of ore in the two mines, and the Pinguico drifts are continuing northward in ore. This proportion of ore, 2,250 feet in 2,650 feet length of openings, is unusual and noteworthy.

ORE SHIPPED

I DO not know what the production of ore in the Carmen has been, as it belongs to another company. The Pinguico has shipped, to the end of October, 1906, 6,350.54 tons of ore. The gross value, by liquidated assays, was $231,070.50, or $36.38 per ton. Some of this ore was sold to smelters, the rest to two small custom mills in the district. The milling has been under the direction of Mr. J. B. Empson, metallurgist to the Guanajuato Development Company, who has developed a very thorough and successful system of treatment. The ore he received averaged $22.45 per ton gross value, and the extraction was $20.34, or 90.6 per cent. In the new mill, which will be adapted closely to the treatment of Pinguico ore, it may be possible to increase this extraction to 92 per cent.

THE NEW MILL

THE new mill will treat 200 tons a day and is expected to beneficiate ore of all grades, so that the heavy costs involved in sending ore to smelters will be avoided. There is still a question whether the rich concentrates can be cyanided, but as the treatment of similar concentrates by this process has been successful in many parts of the world the prospect for similar success at Pinguico is good.

Milling produces 1 per cent. of concentrates worth $1,500.00 per ton and tails which contain 55 per cent. sands and 45 per cent. slimes. The ore has carried $4.25 per ton gold, of which 93.18 per cent. has been recovered; and $18.20 silver, of which 90 per cent. has been extracted. The total extraction, as before said, has been 90.6 per cent., or $20.34 per ton.

MINING AND MILLING COSTS

THE cost of mining and milling is estimated at $4.00, and general expenses and taxes will add about $2.20. The profit as indicated by the four-months' test on ore of the grade treated should, therefore, be above $14.00 per ton, but if all the ores mined had been treated by the new methods the extraction would have been $33.00 per ton and the profit about $25.80. Mr. Empson expects, and I think with reason, to improve the recovery from the slimes somewhat.

The building of a suitable mill will have an important effect upon the mining, increasing materially the amount of ore available from a given vein-area. Lower costs and better extraction make lower-grade ore profitable, and the constitution of the Pinguico vein gives this well-known fact peculiar importance in this mine.

PINGUICO VEIN

THE Pinguico vein is composed of a mass of rock fragments which have been altered to ore by mineralizing solutions. These fragments were formed by faulting and occupy thicknesses reaching up to 9 meters (29 ft.) and more. The mineralization has been intense along one of two lines which constitute what is called distinctively the vein, but the fragments alongside these lines are often well mineralized also, and the width which can be taken out with profit depends upon the cheapness and thoroughness of the extraction in the mill.

All the ore which has been taken out so far, except a small quantity resulting from a cave, has come from four drifts and the winzes which connect them, so that the full thickness of the vein has not been developed as it would have been by stoping. When the new mill is in operation it will probably be found that the thickness of ore mined will exceed considerably that now measured in the drifts, which Mr. Wiltsee gives as 4.9 meters, or 16 ft.

CHARACTERISTICS OF THE MINE

ONE of the characteristics of this mine is the existence of a leached zone at the top of the vein 250 feet deep. Besides this the vein is covered by layers of barren rock which has been removed only partially by erosion. The material leached from the upper part of the vein was carried down and redeposited at lower levels. Apparently the mine is entering upon one of the most important of these enriched zones at depths over 500 feet below the surface, since the winzes below the 125-meter level show a strong improvement in value.

There appear to be two levels at which this improvement in grade is found, the 111-meter and below the 125-meter level. These depths are measured from the tunnel where the south shaft was sunk; and this being 53 meters below the surface, that quantity should be added to the figures given for the levels to ascertain the true depth.

MEAN VALUES OF SAMPLES

THE enrichment is shown by the following mean values of the samples taken on each level:

		(Top of Ore.) From Surface
73 meter level (237 ft.)	410 ft. = $4.70 per ton
103 " " (335 ")	510 " = 9.81 " "
111 " " (363 ")	535 " = 46.45 " "
117 " " (380 ")	554 " = 25.63 " "
125 " " (407 ")	584 " = 22.16 " "
Winzes 60 ft.	
under 125 level (467 ")	650 " = 53.00 " "

The irregularity shown is due partly to the different lengths of the openings named, a short and a long drift not being directly comparable on account of the different number of samples.

The fact of increase in value below the depth of 500 feet seems to be established; and as it has continued for 50 feet in depth and seems to be still going on, the effect upon the calculation of future reserves is very great. Mr. Wiltsee's report enters minutely into these calculations. What facts are known indicate that the 145-150-meter level will have nearly two and a half times the value of the 125-level if the ore maintains its length and thickness, about which no doubt is felt. The 125 level is already considerably longer in ore than when Mr. Wiltsee's visit ended, and the prospect is that it and the level below it will be longer still.

HISTORY OF PINGUICO VEIN

THE facts I have given enable us to read the history of the Pinguico vein with considerable accuracy. Guanajuato has been a region of long-continued and intense volcanic activity. Originally composed of sedimentary rocks, schists, limestones, etc., these have been so completely buried that only a small triangular area of them north of the town is known.

All the rest of the isolated Guanajuato Mountains is composed of eruptive rocks, the character and laminated condition of which point to successive flows over a surface and, in case of the so-called "conglomerate," into water.

One of the most massive of these flows was the Pinguico rhyolite. Great faulting followed and probably accompanied in part these outpourings of rock; and the mother-vein of the district, the Veta Madre, is in a fault that breaks through the sedimentary rocks, the conglomerate and the rhyolite which lie on them.

FAULTING MOVEMENTS

THE Veta Madre shows us that the Pinguico rhyolite is the second of the eruptives in age and it has participated in most, if not all, of the faulting movements which have given the district its present form. It is clear that faulting of the greatest importance took place after the Veta Madre was partially formed. At the Pinguico a profound crack was broken in the hanging wall of the mother-lode, and the block between the two fractures slipped down and by wedging action produced great crushing in the Pinguico.

The breaking of the rhyolite down to the line of the mother-lode permitted the ore solutions which formed the Veta Madre to enter the Pinguico also and change the broken fragments in the fault to ore.

LEACHING

THERE is good reason for believing that after the vein was formed it was exposed to the atmosphere and leached in the upper 250 feet, just as we find veins leached which are now exposed to the air and rain. No doubt there was erosion also that planed off the rhyolite, but there is no indication of its amount.

Finally the leached outcrop of the vein was covered by new flows of rocks, and

then, I think, commenced a new and peculiar process. The vein seems to have been steeped in water, which dissolved such substances as lime and alumina, leaving an unusually large proportion of small open spaces in the upper levels and producing a remarkably liquid clay well known to the Mexicans and called by them "jaboncilla." This clay is always rich in the bullion metals.

The rocks which were formed over the Veta Madre and the Pinguico and other veins were also flows of considerable thickness, several hundred feet at least, and their erosion has produced the surface of the present day.

PERMANENCE OF VEIN

EVERY fact known indicates great permanence for the Pinguico vein. Undoubtedly it occupies a fault which breaks through the hanging wall of the great Veta Madre, which has been the source of the immense production of this district, estimated at a thousand million dollars.

The Veta Madre is nearly parallel to and about 5,000 feet east of the Pinguico vein and it has a dip of forty to forty-five degrees toward Pinguico. The faulting in this district is known to have been very profound, and it is entirely probable that the Pinguico fault extends down to the mother-vein, 4,000 or more feet below. The situation is similar to that of the Comstock lode in Nevada, where the Comstock vein is a fault fissure in the hanging wall of the underlying Virginia vein. The difference in the two situations is that the Virginia vein was not profitable above its junction with the vein in its own hanging wall, while here that part of the long mother-lode which is opposite the Pinguico has good ore and valuable mines. Still this southern part of the Veta Madre has not been so productive as the northern end and it may be that the Pinguico has, to some extent, robbed the Veta Madre. If so, the history of the great productive districts, Guanajuato and the Comstock, have points of parallelism that were not suspected until the Pinguico vein was opened.

SUMMARIZATION

TO sum up, the Pinguico vein as shown in its existing openings is a fault fissure in a heavy bed of rhyolite which is known to be 675 feet thick and may reach 1,500–1,700 feet in thickness. It forms a great flow which extends for two miles N. 40° W. from the Carmen tunnel, and where the covering rocks have been eroded it shows a width of 5,000 feet. This must be one of the great members of the Guanajuato series, for the dimensions given merely measure what can be seen on the surface. Before the country was altered by faulting and erosion, this mass of rhyolite probably covered the surface for many miles in every direction. Its thickness cannot be ascertained with accuracy, but was probably 1,500 feet, and two-thirds of this, or 1,000 feet, still lies below the lowest workings of the mine.

The character of this underlying rock is just as favorable to the formation of ore as that part which the mine has opened already. The volcanic "conglomerate" is supposed to underlie the rhyolite at Pinguico, as elsewhere in the district.

PRESENT CONDITION

THERE is no doubt that the present condition of the Pinguico is that of a remarkably valuable mine with a well-assured future of the greatest promise. The elements which have entered into its formation are the most permanent known in mining. It occurs in a region which has been pronounced to be the greatest mining district in the world and to which the most careful authorities have accredited an immense production of gold and silver. The improvements in methods of extraction have given a thoroughness and certainty to the treatment of its ores that are greater than ever before, and at the same time the introduction of electrical power in quantity sufficient for the whole camp has both cheapened this heavy item of expense and given trustworthiness to the calculations of cost.

PROFITS

IT is reasonably certain that a vein of the size and character of Pinguico can be mined and milled for the costs given above, and it is equally certain that ores of the value found by the sale of 6,000 tons will give the profit indicated by treatment in the large way. The mine of the present day ought to give the profit shown by Mr. Wiltsee, less about one dollar per ton for general expenses, and this deduction has been compensated by the increased length of drifts in ore since the date of his report and by other improvements.

Mr. Wiltsee's computations extended to the depth of 208 meters from the surface, but only eighty-two meters of that was ore-bearing, the remainder being leached. There remains thirty-six meters to the level of the Carmen lower tunnel, and while the value of that yet unopened ground cannot be estimated closely it is likely to double Mr. Wiltsee's estimates from ore in sight. That is equivalent to saying that the next thirty-six meters of depth will equal in productiveness the eighty-two meters of ore through which the mine has penetrated already, and every fact that has been collected supports that belief unreservedly. There can be no doubt that the Pinguico is a mine of very great merit.

(Signed)   JOHN A. CHURCH, E.M.

Mining Engineer.

Guanajuato, Mex., November 5, 1906.

REPORT OF A. B. CARPENTER, E.M.

Mr. Carpenter is a well-known Mining Engineer, who has been actively engaged in mine examinations in the Republic of Mexico for some years, and is thoroughly familiar with existing conditions in that mining field. Graduating from Beloit College, Wisconsin, in 1893, after taking a post-graduate course in geology and mineralogy in the same college, he entered the Michigan College of Mines at Houghton, Mich., obtaining the degree of Sc.B. and E.M. His initial mining engagement was in the Cripple Creek District as Mining Engineer and Assayer, with later experience in Victor, Colo. Transferring his operations to the Chihuahua field, he began an active career in the Republic of Mexico, soon after becoming identified with the Mexican Gold and Silver Recovery Company, which has carried on extensive operations in the Mexican field. Mr. Carpenter became a specialist in the examination of mining properties, and in that capacity was constantly employed in the investigation and examination of mines for several years. His experience and success in this particular branch of mine engineering place him in the foremost rank as a mining authority in the Republic of Mexico.

Report upon the Properties of
THE PINGUICO MINES COMPANY
By A. B. Carpenter, E.M.

Introduction—Development Work—Shoots of Rich Ore—Values Increase with Depth—Summary of Condition—Best Showing of any Mine.

INTRODUCTION

I PRESENT herewith a general statement relative to the work as it has been carried on in the Pinguico Mine since the acquisition of that property by your Company in April of the present year, together with my opinion of the present prospects of the property.

DEVELOPMENT WORK

THE development work has been under my supervision as Consulting Engineer during this time, and it is a matter of a great deal of pride and satisfaction that—notwithstanding the very adverse conditions under which the work has had to be carried on, with hoisting and pumping facilities far below the necessary requirements—so gratifying a showing has been made in a period of but six months, the first half of which was necessarily devoted to modernly equipping and preparing the mine for rapid development. At the time of the purchase of the property, but one single ore shoot had been discovered and worked and it was in the general characteristics of this shoot, its persistence and improvement, both in value and in width, as depth was attained, as also the regular occurrence of such shoots in the adjoining "El Carmen" Mine, that we adjudged the property worth the purchase price and anticipated its development into a most valuable mining proposition.

SHOOTS OF RICH ORE

THE development work that has been done since has given results far in excess of my most sanguine expectations. Shoots of rich ore have succeeded each other with a regularity not known in the adjoining property. It has been my privilege, during my visit to the property at this time, to have gone into the matter of present ore reserves and the result of the development of the property to date, with Mr. E. A. Wiltsee, who is now reporting on the property for you, and we have together based the present estimate of value and tonnage of ore on our intimate knowledge of the character of the ore bodies as we know them to be, restricting ourselves, however, to what we know are safe and conservative limits outside present actual developments. Our measurements and calculations as embodied in Mr. Wiltsee's report give a tonnage of available ore at this date to be 60,667 tons, with a gross value of $2,101,906.75 U. S. Cy. Considering that at the time of the purchase of the property there was estimated to be but 8,935 tons in sight with a gross value of $258,760.00 gold, the showing is certainly most satisfactory and unusual.

VALUES INCREASE WITH DEPTH

HOWEVER, under present conditions, though not yet by any means the best, we can assure you that the development during the next few months will be much more rapid than any previous record. If the ore shoots continue as persistent—and there is nothing that appears now which would lead us to believe that they will not only continue, but improve—a remarkable additional tonnage and value can be anticipated. As an example of such ore increase, a result of the prosecution of the points of development now in hand, may be stated roughly as follows, viz., by sinking winze No. 1, estimating the width of ore thus developed to be the average width of blocks "E" and "E-1" (4 meters), in each meter increase in depth in the winze (an average day's work) will add a tonnage of 818 tons to blocks "K," "E," and "E-1." Taking the value of this increase to be the average value of the blocks—$58.53 for blocks "E" and "E-1," and $38.02 for block "K"—the gross value of ore by one meter's sinking in the winze amounts to $40,400 U. S. Cy. As, however, the ore shows that its value has increased with depth in the winze until at the present time it is running approximately $124.00 per ton, should we assume the values in the bottom of the block to be as good as in the present bottom of the winze, or even reduce it to $80.00 for conservatism, the gross value of increase can be considered to be approximately $50,000.00 for each meter sunk. We can in a similar manner compute the ore increase as a result of the drivage of the north drift on the 125-meter level beyond blocks "J" and "N." This level has just passed through a pinch in the vein and is now again in a wide ore shoot of good grade (see Longitudinal Section, appendix to Mr. Wiltsee's report). Taking as the width of this ore shoot the average width of the last shoot passed through and a safe assumption that the same grade of ore extends ten meters below and above the level, we can state that every two meters of advance (which is the amount driven in this drift per day) will put in sight 503 tons of ore. As the ore now in the face carries a value of approximately $25.00 per ton, each day's advance in this drift at the present time is increasing the gross value of the ore reserves by $12,650.00. These above figures allow the general statement that the work in the mine, at these two points of development only, is at the present time placing between $53,050.00 and $62,-650.00 U. S. Cy. gross value of ore in sight per day.

Owing to inadequate hoisting facilities the present development work in the mine is restricted mainly to the sinking of winzes No. 1 and No. 2 below the 125-meter level and the driving north alone

the 125-meter level. Besides this, as opportunity allows, the 103-meter level is continued north, and an intermediate level is being run to assist the ventilation of the mine.

As I expect that Mr. Wiltsee will cover all of the principal points of development and possibilities of the mine, I shall conclude with the statement that I consider the salient features of the present Pinguico proposition to be as follows:

SUMMARY OF CONDITIONS

AN extensive property of 300 acres with a length on a practically virgin vein of 8,200 feet.

The lowest present level of the mine shows the average of the vein throughout an entire length of 600 feet to run better than $50.00 U. S. Cy. per ton.

Ore bodies, that have shown in the development that has been done on them so far, to be of unusually high grade.

That the shoots are persistent and tend to widen in depth with ore of increased value.

That a succession of ore shoots has already been proved, for a distance of 215 meters (705 ft.) in the Pinguico property, and within that distance they have been demonstrated to be of greater extent than those in the adjoining property.

That the extremely soft and broken character of the ore of the vein will allow its extraction by modern methods at a most economical cost.

That the treatment of these ores during the past four months at the Nayal and Central mills by concentrating and cyaniding has clearly demonstrated that extractions of above 90 per cent. of the total values can be obtained at the general low cost for such treatment.

BEST SHOWING OF ANY MINE

FINALLY, with these favorable conditions that have already been proved to exist, with ore of such value and quantity opened up on less than one-tenth of the total length of vein embraced within the limits of the property, the future of the Pinguico Mines

Company is exceedingly bright, and the Guanajuato Development Company is to be congratulated in having developed a mine which for the amount of work done certainly has a better showing than any mine that it has ever been my fortune to have previously seen.

Respectfully submitted,

ALVIN B. CARPENTER, E.M.

Guanajuato, Mex., Oct. 22, 1906.

REPORT OF J. B. EMPSON, E.M.

Mr. Empson is a Metallurgical Engineer of large experience, having been connected with important milling properties in various parts of the world. He is a graduate from the Thames School of Mines in New Zealand. He began his mining career in 1893, in charge of a cyanide tailings proposition in Australia, after which he was foreman of the "Woodstock Mill" in New Zealand (an 80-ton mill), and for the past twelve years has made a specialty of cyanidation of both gold and silver ores, having been in charge of several mills in the United States, prominent among which may be mentioned the Dakota Mining & Milling Company (capacity, 100 tons per day), the "Gilt Edge" Cyanide Mill (a 120-ton mill), both located in the Black Hills District—his connection with the last two covering a period of six years.

It is a noteworthy fact that the mills under Mr. Empson's supervision attained a greater extraction at a smaller cost than any of the mills in the Black Hills District, with the possible exception of the "Homestake" Mills, whose treatment costs are based upon handling 4,000 tons of ore per day.

The value of his experience in a camp where the average grade of ore was but $2.50 to $3.00 U. S. Cy. per ton, necessitating the utmost economy in milling costs, can readily be recognized in a camp like Guanajuato, where the cyanidation of ores is yet in its infancy and average milling costs yet to be established.

Report upon the Properties of
THE PINGUICO MINES COMPANY
By J. B. Empson, E.M.

ORE GANGUE

CONSISTS of Silica (SiO_2), Kaolin (hydrated silicate of alumina), Carbonate of Lime, Iron (principally as a sulphide), Arsenopyrite, Manganese, Silver (as sulphide, chloride, and in combination with arsenic and iron), and Gold: forming a soft honeycombed quartz, impregnated with bands and spots of silver sulphide and carrying a large proportion of white clay or kaolin.

BY ANALYSIS

	Per Cent.
Silica (SiO_2)	} 93.6
Insol. matter and Kaolin..	
Iron	1.2
Lime (calcium)	.56
Manganese	1.1
Sulphur	.97
Silver	920 grams per ton
Gold	6 " " "
Arsenic	} trace
Antimony	

VALUES

THE values are in Gold and Silver. GOLD occurs free in small amounts (about 1 gram per ton of ore being amenable to amalgamation). The balance of the gold values are in extremely fine particles, easily attacked by cyanide solution. Gold is also present combined with the Pyrites.

SILVER occurs mainly in the form of Argentite (AgS_2), which carries 87 per cent. of silver. Also in the form of Cerargyrite, Proustite, and Pyrargyrite.

TREATMENT

THE cyanide mills at "La Central" and "Nayal," both under my personal supervision, have been treating Pinguico ore for the last four months with results—checked against by bullion returns—as shown below.

Both mills consist at present of ten stamps (now being increased), weight 850 lbs. each, 5" drop, 104 drops per minute. Screen used: No. 30 mesh, 31 wire.

The ore is crushed in the batteries with water at a ratio of 9.5 tons of water to one ton of ore.

Pulp is concentrated on No. 5 Wilfley tables and canvas tables, giving as a product 1.07 per cent. of the total ore.

Heretofore the high-grade ores have been shipped to the smelters, leaving the average grade of the ore milled $18.20 silver and $4.25 gold—total $22.45 U. S. Cy. Average grade of concentrates from Wilfley tables $1,500.00 per ton, and from canvas tables $550.00 per ton.

After concentration and classification, sands go to treatment in sand tanks, and slimes in slime tanks in the proportion of 55 per cent. sands and 45 per cent. slimes.

Precipitation on zinc is 98 per cent. of the contents of the solution.

With reference to sizing of material, see sizing tests attached.

SUMMARY OF SAVING

	Gold Per Ct.	Silver Per Ct.	Total Per Ct.
Concentration	61.9	50.03	52.25
Extraction from sands	19.28	21.98	21.47
" " slimes	12.00	17.99	16.88
Total	93.18	90.	90.60

It must be borne in mind that the above figures represent the average of actual results obtained in the treatment of Pinguico ores in the "Nayal" and "La Central" mills, neither of which are particularly adapted for their treatment, both being custom mills treating all the various ores of the camp, without special adaptation to any.

The above summary of saving in these mills, however, proves conclusively that the Pinguico ores are ideal for cyanidation, are remarkably free from substances deleterious to cyanide, and can be treated at an exceedingly low cost (referred to in detail later on in this report).

In the new mill now being designed by me, for the special treatment of the Pinguico ores, I am confident that an extraction of upwards of 93 per cent. of the total contents of the silver and gold will be secured.

NEW MILL FOR PINGUICO ORE

THE new mill for Pinguico is designed to crush and treat 200 tons per day, divided into two units of 100 tons each, viz.: 1 crusher, 20 stamps, and 1 Chilean mill to each unit.

Ore is to be received over aerial tram line from the mine, situated about one-half mile from the site of the mill. Crusher floor is ninety meters below the hoist at the mine. Ample crusher floor room is provided.

Ore is received in a bin on crusher floor by the automatic dumping of the cable buckets. From this bin it is trammed to the mill and dumped on a floor over the ore bins, where the coarse rock is picked out and crushed through two 9" x 15" Blake crushers, the gouge or fine rock going through shoveling holes into the bins; lime to be added at the same time, in proper proportion.

Ore from bins about 2" size goes by means of Challenge self-feeders to forty stamps, weight 1,050 lbs., 5" drop, 102 drops per minute; mortars, narrow type, heavy base. Screens on mortars 4 mesh, No. 14 wire. Capacity per stamp estimated at 5 tons per 24 hours.

Pulp from stamps goes to trough classifiers, with shallow pockets at bottom, giving a rough classification between ¼ mesh to 30 mesh.

All product coarser than 30 mesh goes to two modern high-speed Chilean mills, each with a capacity of from sixty-five to seventy-five tons per day, to 30 mesh. From the sizing tests on the Pinguico ores as shown by the sheets attached to this report, it is clearly evident that the ore need not be crushed to finer than 30 mesh.

Pulp from Chilean mills, together with overflow from trough classifiers, goes to distributing boxes, and from there to the Wilfley concentrators.

Middlings from Wilfley concentrators to be reground in a small mill and reconcentrated on four more Wilfley concentrators.

Total product of Wilfleys to go to mechanical classifiers, giving a clean product of sand and slime; sands going direct to sand tanks, and slime to canvas or cement tables especially designed for taking out the fine sulphides. Tailings from these tables go to slime-thickening tanks designed to give clear water overflow for mill use and thick slime for treatment in slime tanks, of which there are twelve 30' diameter x 12' deep, all connected by centrifugal pump for agitation.

Solution from slime tanks goes to filter tanks, and so to zinc boxes, where values are precipitated.

All concentrates from Wilfley concentrators and canvas or cement tables go to a concentrate room where concentrates are drained, ready to ship or treat.

Experiments are well in hand to treat the concentrates by cyanide and thus save the smelter charges.

ESTIMATED COSTS OF OPERATING NEW MILL
(Per Ton of Ore)

	U. S. Cy.
Power	$0.28
Cyanide and chemicals	.50
Zinc	.05
Labor	.10
Wear and repairs	.25
Administration	.20
Interest on investment	.15
Depreciation	.15
Sundries	.10
Total cost per ton	$1.78 U. S. Cy.

The above description of this mill is accompanied by detailed plans and drawings which show the complete design for the new Pinguico mill of a capacity of 200 tons per day, which will cost, when completed and ready to run, not exceeding $150,000.00 U. S. Cy.

Respectfully submitted,

(Signed) J. B. EMPSON, E.M.

Guanajuato, Mex., Oct. 25, 1906.

SIZING TESTS—PINGUICO ORE

BATTERY HEADS					SAND TAILINGS				
Number of Mesh	Weight in Grams	Percent-age	Assay in Grams		Number of Mesh	Weight in Grams	Percent-age	Assay in Grams	
			Silver	Gold				Silver	Gold
On 40	35	3.5			On 40	35	3.5	37	.02
" 60	110	11.	411	4	" 60	332	33.2	50	.01
" 80	125	12.5	719	3	" 80	262	26.2	49	.025
" 100	130	13.	648	7	" 100	82	8.2	55	.02
" 120	100	10.	679	6	" 120	182	18.2	60	.02
" 200	50	5.	750	5	" 200	54	5.4	58	.02
Through 200	450	45.	1157	8.5	Through 200	53	5.3	45	.02
	1000	100.	925	5.99		1000	100.	52	.02

From the above sizing tests, it is clearly evident that the ore need not be crushed finer than 30 mesh—31 wire.

REPORT BY GEO. W. BRYANT

Mr. Bryant is a practical mining man and mine operator of long experience and proved capacity for large mining operations. He has been actively engaged as a mine manager, business manager, and in other executive positions for the past thirteen years, operating upwards of twenty mining properties in the Guanajuato Camp. Beginning his mining career in Mexico as an accountant and business manager for properties controlled by the United Mexican Mines Association, Ltd., London, he afterwards became resident manager for that corporation. Following this, he became manager of the Victoria Mines Company, and later had charge of the San Prospero Mines, the Peregrina Mines, the Refugio Mines, the Aparecida Mines, the La Central Groups, and many other successful properties in the Guanajuato Camp.

Mr. Bryant is widely and favorably known in mining circles throughout Mexico as a mine manager. His intimate knowledge of the Pinguico properties, coupled with his successful experience as a practical mining man, insures an intelligent and successful operation of this exceptional property, with the management placed in his hands.

Report upon the Properties of
THE PINGUICO MINES COMPANY
By Geo. W. Bryant

Introduction—Results in Three Months—Tremendous Ore Bodies—Geological Indication $2,000,000 per year for 20 years—The Mill—Daily Profit—Interest and Reinvestment Account.

INTRODUCTION

THE reports rendered to you by Messrs. Wiltsee and Carpenter on the present condition of the Pinguico Mine are so complete that but little remains for me to say.

Mr. J. B. EMPSON, our Consulting Metallurgist, has fully dealt with the results obtained from treating the ores in the small cyanide plants at present devoted to that purpose.

When recommending this property to the Guanajuato Development Company in February, 1906, I stated that six months' work would put in sight $1,225,-000.00 U. S. Cy., while by the reports of Messrs. Wiltsee and Carpenter $2,100,000.00 U. S. Cy. are now measurable without considering the speculative value of the property.

RESULTS IN THREE MONTHS

WE obtained possession of the property in April of the present year.

Three months were occupied in putting the mine in shape and proper condition for development. The work of the last three months has been so rapid, as a consequence of this preparatory work, that the results obtained have been in excess of my calculations.

As conservative Mining Engineers, Messrs. Wiltsee and Carpenter are confined to reporting upon absolutely available ore, and are prohibited from passing upon the future value of the property.

As I am very largely interested personally in the mine, and expect to profit largely by its success, I am not disposed to deceive myself as to its future and I am not forced to confine my estimates to the actual ore measurable upon four opened sides, but, on the contrary, can give you and my fellow-shareholders a business opinion of the value of this property.

During the past ten years I have carefully studied the various ore occurrences of the Guanajuato Mining District, from which there have been extracted during the last three centuries more than one billion dollars in silver and gold.

A single ore body in the Valenciana Mine yielded $300,000,000.00, another in La Luz yielded $120,000,000.00, several others in various parts of the camp have yielded from $25,000,000.00 to $50,-000,000.00.

In Pinguico we have opened up over $2,000,000.00 in about three months, and as the entire floor of the bottom level of the mine is in much higher grade ore than the blocks measured and calculated by Messrs. Wiltsee and Carpenter, it becomes of great interest to the owners of the property to make a comparison between our property and the famous mines just mentioned.

TREMENDOUS ORE BODIES?

THE Valenciana and La Luz ore bodies were hidden below surface at a depth of about five hundred feet—scarcely any values reaching surface.

In Pinguico similar conditions obtain. Our ore does not reach within three hundred feet of surface, but from that point downwards the deposit steadily widens and grows richer.

The material comprising the ore of the Pinguico vein bears a startling resemblance to the soft material of La Luz and Valenciana, which so greatly assisted the miners of bygone days in extracting vast sums of money from their mines without the aid of modern machinery or explosives.

While the rock in which the Pinguico ore occurs is not entirely similar in character to that in which the better known bonanzas have been found, yet it is of the same eruptive period, and, having been tremendously fractured and fissured by mechanical strains, it has furnished channels for mineralizing solutions in exactly the same manner as Valenciana and La Luz.

GEOLOGICAL INDICATION

OUR geological investigations clearly demonstrate that the rock in which our known ore body occurs reaches a depth of many thousand feet below our present workings. It can be readily assumed that this rock was forced up from below by enormous pressure and that, as it was forced up, it displaced overlying rocks whose tremendous weight exercised a counter-pressure, the result being cracking, fracturing, and fissuring of the entire mass.

The heated solutions carrying gold, silver, sulphur, and iron were forced up into the cracked mass from still greater depths and deposited their minerals in the open cracks and fissures, and in their superheated condition even penetrated into the solid rock—thus forming what we consider to-day as the Pinguico vein.

The depth to which its mineralization may reach is only limited to the depth of the mass of rock in which the Pinguico vein and its feeding channels occur.

As previously stated, this depth is known to be many thousand feet.

The Valenciana and La Luz ore bodies, occurring under similar conditions, were followed to a depth of 1,500 feet from their apex, and the bottoms of both mines were left in good ore.

There is every reason to calculate upon at least equal depth for the Pinguico ore body.

$2,000,000 PER YEAR FOR 20 YEARS

THE present length of the Pinguico ore body is almost eight hundred feet and it continues in good ore laterally. Should it reach the same lateral extension as the Valenciana and La Luz ore bodies, viz., about four thousand feet, and attain equal depth while retaining its present average value, the production could not fail to be not less than $2,000,000.00 per year for the next twenty years.

By January 1st, 1907, the present Pinguico shaft will be equipped with a 50-H. P. electric hoist and two electric pumps, permitting an extraction of about 200 tons of ore per day from this shaft. This will permit an advance in development work through this shaft of about fifty feet daily or nearly three times as much as is at present being accomplished.

By March 1st, 1907, the No. 3 Carmen tunnel, which has been driven three thousand feet towards the Pinguico end line, will reach our property and, by draining and ventilating our mine at a point 205 feet below our bottom level, will greatly expedite the opening up of our mine.

Also about March 1st, 1907, our Fortuna shaft will have reached sufficient depth to connect with our present 125-meter level, and will therefore be in the ore body. This shaft is now equipped with a double drum electric hoist and a 3-drill electrically driven air compressor, with which equipment it will handle about 200 tons of ore per day. At present about sixty tons of ore are extracted daily and are being sold at exorbitant treatment charges to the only available purchasers, viz., small custom mills in the vicinity and the smelter at Aguascalientes.

This ore, in spite of high treatment charges, pays all costs of construction, operation, development, etc., and leaves a profit of from $5,000.00 to $10,000.00 per month, while every month sees additional ore blocked out having a value of from $300,000.00 to $600,000.00.

The 400 tons extracted daily next year should have a value of about $10,-000.00 per day. Sufficient of this will be sold to pay all expenses, and the remainder kept for treatment in the Company's own mill, which should be ready about January 1st, 1908.

THE MILL

MR. EMPSON'S report described the mill in full. If fairly quick deliveries of material and machinery can be obtained from factories, it should be ready before January, 1908.

The opportunity afforded Mr. Empson, our metallurgist, of testing the Pinguico ores by constantly treating them, during the past four months, in the mills under his charge, has been a great assistance in determining the type of mill to be adopted and the manner of treatment, and will save the Company large amounts of money in constructing their mill.

Until recently the ore was considered difficult to treat by cyaniding, but constant experiment and practice under Mr. Empson's supervision have demonstrated the contrary, and the ore, properly treated, proves extremely docile, yielding high extraction at low cost.

The mill will treat 200 tons per day of ore worth about $35.00 U. S. Cy., of which about $26.00 U. S. Cy. will be silver and $9.00 U. S. Cy. gold.

The saving in the new mill will be about 90 per cent. of the silver and 94 per cent. of the gold, or a total saving of 91 per cent. of the combined values.

The present Government taxes on bullion produced are 4⅜ per cent. of its value.

The cost of marketing the bullion is about 1¼ per cent. of its value.

The cost of mining, transportation to mill, and milling will be about $4.00 per metric ton.

General expenses of all kinds may add $1.00 per ton to these costs.

The following table shows value of ore per ton as mined, deduction for losses in milling, taxes, marketing charges, mining

costs, transportation to mill, milling costs, and general expenses:

		U. S. Cy.
Value of one metric ton as mined		$35.00
9 per cent. loss in milling	$3.15	
6 per cent. taxes and marketing bullion (calculated on $31.85 produced)	1.91	
Mining cost	2.00	
Milling, including transportation	2.00	
General expenses	1.00	10.06
Net profit per metric ton		$24.94

The mill as designed will have a minimum daily capacity of two hundred metric tons, and its daily product and profit will be as follows:

Two hundred tons introduced at $35.00	$7,000.00
Deductions for losses, taxes, marketing, mining, transportation, milling and general expenses:	
Two hundred tons at $10.06	$2,012.00
Daily profit	$4,988.00
About 300 working days can be figured on, giving a yearly profit of	$1,500,000.00

which, according to the by-laws of the Company, would be divided as follows:

6 per cent. interest Preferred stock	$120,000.00	
50 per cent. of the remainder for the retirement of the Preferred	690,000.00	
Available for common stock dividends	690,000.00	
		$1,500,000.00

By the time the mill is ready I feel certain that at least 300,000 tons of ore will be actually blocked out, with an equal quantity of probable ore in sight, thereby assuring ten years' mill-run. From present indications it is probable that the grade will be higher than that calculated upon, rather than lower.

INTEREST AND RETIREMENT ACCOUNTS

IN three years the interest and retirement accounts will have been suspended by the entire reimbursement of Preferred stock and the net earnings will be entirely applicable to dividends on common stock.

The saving to the Company by milling its own ores is shown by the fact that a ton of $35.00 ore sold under best market conditions to-day yields only $15.00, while $25.00 is yielded in the Company's own mill. This difference of $10.00 per ton means $50,000.00 per month saved by milling in the Company's own mill. The mill costs about $150,000.00, so that in three months its cost will have been returned to the Company through the saving over present conditions of ore selling.

The sale of Preferred stock provides for a working capital of $210,000.00. Of this $150,000.00 will be used for mill, $10,000 for a dam and necessary pipe line, and $25,000.00 for an aerial cable connecting shafts with mill site, about three-quarters of a mile distant. As all development and equipment of mine costs are paid out of present production, the balance of $25,000.00 will furnish mill supplies and will build necessary houses for employes, warehouses, etc.

Respectfully submitted,

(Signed)   **GEO. W. BRYANT,**
General Manager.

Guanajuato, Mex., October 29, 1906.